1

TRACING AND COLORING

SHORTER BAPTIST

CATECHISM

WORKBOOK

A creative way of keeping your children
involved in learning the catechism .

EDITORIAL CREDO

Toda la vida para la gloria de Dios

Credo
Editorial

Q. 1 **Why should my parents instruct me in the word of God?**

A. Because God commands it.

PROVE IT !

Deut. 6: 6-7

Q.2

Who created you?

A.

_____

PROVE IT !

Genesis 1:27

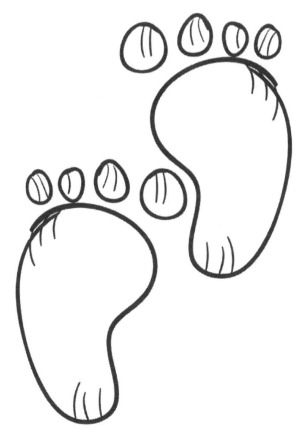

Q.3

What else did God create?

A.

All things.

_____

PROVE IT !

Genesis 1:1

Q. 4

Why did God create all things and us?

A.

For His own Glory.

PROVE IT !

Romans 11:36

Q.5
How can we glorify God?
A.

Loving and obeying
Him.

PROVE IT !
Deuteronomy 6:5-6

Q.6
Why should we glorify God?

A. He created and takes care of me.

PROVE IT !

Revelation 4:11

Q.7 **Where do we learn to glorify God ?**

A.

Only the Bible.

PROVE IT !

Psalm 119:9

Q.8

What does the Bible teach us ?

A. Who is God and His commands.

PROVE IT !

2 Timothy 3:16-17

Q.9
Who wrote the Holy Bible?

A. Holy man by the
Holy Spirit
_____
PROVE IT !
2 Peter 1:21

Q.10

What is God?

A. Spirit, not with human body.

PROVE IT !

John 4:24

Q.11
Is there more than one God?

A. No, there is only one God.

PROVE IT !
Isaiah 44:6b

Q.12

In how many person does God exist?

A.

In 3 persons

PROVE IT !

2 Corinthians 13:14

Q.13   # Who are they?

A.   Father, Son,

Holy Spirit.

PROVE IT !
Matthew 28:19

Q.14   # Where is God?

A.

God is everywhere

PROVE IT!

Psalm 139:7-8

Q.15 **Can we see God?**

A. No, I cannot, but he can see me all the time.

PROVE IT!

John 1:18a

Q. 16

Does God know all things ?

A. Yes, nothing can be hidden from God.

PROVE IT !

Hebrews 4:13

Q. 17 **Can God do all things?**

A. Yes, God does all

His holy will.

PROVE IT !

Mark 10:27

Q. 18

Who are our first parents?

A.

Adam and Eve .

PROVE IT !

Genesis 2:7, 22

Q. 19
What were our first parents made of?

A.   Adam from the ground. Eve from Adam's body

PROVE IT !
Genesis 2:7/22

Q.20

In what condition did God make Adam and Eve?

A.

Made them Holy and
Happy .

PROVE IT !

Ecclesiastes 7:29

Q.21

What relationship did Adam have with God. ?

A.   A Sonship

relationship.

PROVE IT !

Luke 3:38

Q. 22

What commandment did God give Adam?

A.

Obey God perfectly

PROVE IT !

Genesis 2:16-17

Q. 23   **What did God promise Adam?**

A.   If Adam obeyed God would reward him with life.

PROVE IT !

Genesis 2: 16-17

Q. 24

What threat did God make to Adam?

A.

Adam would be
punished with death

PROVE IT !
Genesis 2: 16-17

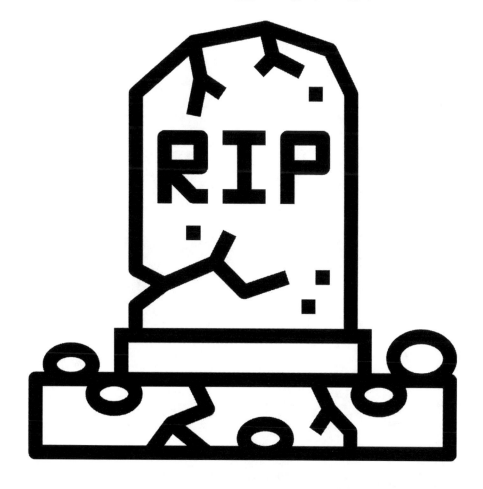

Q.25   **Did Adam obey God?**

A.

No, Adam sinned
against God.

PROVE IT !
Genesis 3:6

Q. 26

What is sin ?

A. Breaking God's Law

Transgression of the Law of God.

PROVE IT !
1 John 3:4

Q.27 **What do we mean by breaking God's law?**

A. Not doing what he commands us to do.

PROVE IT!

James 2:17

Q.28 **What do we understand by transgression?**

A. Do what God forbids.

PROVE IT !

James 2:10

Q.29

What was the first sin of our first parents?

A.

Eating from the
forbidden tree

PROVE IT!

Genesis 3:6

Q.30 Who tempted them to sin?

A. Devil tempted Eve and she gave Adam to eat.

PROVE IT !
Genesis 3:4-5

Q. 31 What happened to our first parents when they sinned?

A.

They became sinful and miserable

PROVE IT !

Romans 5:12

Q. 33 **What effect does Adam's sin have on everyone?**

A. We were born in sin and in the state of misery.

PROVE IT!

Ephesians 2:3b

Q.35 **Did God let all of us fall into the state of sin and misery?**

A. No, God purposed to save his people by sending a Redeemer

PROVE IT !

Ephesians 1:4-5

Q. 37

Who is Jesus Christ?

A. The eternal Son of God.

PROVE IT !

John 20:31

37

Q. 38

How did Christ redeem his people?

A.

He obeyed and suffered punishment of sin.

PROVE IT !

Romans 5:18

Q. 39

How did He suffer and obey for His people?

A.

Became Man to obey and suffered punishment.

PROVE IT !

Hebrews 2:14

Q. 40 **How did the Son of God become Man?**

A.

He was born to a virgin woman named Mary.

PROVE IT !
Matthew 1:18

Q. 41

Has the Lord Jesus Christ ever sinned like all other men?

A.

No, He is Holy, blameless, and pure.

PROVE IT !

Hebrews 7:26

Q. 42

What offices does Christ hold?

A.

Prophet, Priest, and King

PROVE IT !

Revelations 1:5

Q.43

How is Christ a prophet?

A. He teaches us the will God.

PROVE IT !

Acts 3:22

Q. 44

How is Christ a priest?

A.

Died for our sins
_____

PROVE IT !

Romans 8:34

44

Q. 45

How is Christ King?

A.

He rules over us and
defends us.

PROVE IT !

1 Corinthians 15:25

Q. 46 **Why do we need Christ as a prophet?**

A. Because I am Ignorant

PROVE IT !

Romans 3:11

46

Q. 47 Why do we need Christ as a Priest?

A. Because I am guilty

PROVE IT !

Romans 3:23

Q. 48 **Why do we need Christ as King?**

A. I am helpless and weak.

PROVE IT !
Psalm 56:3

Q.49

What kind of life did Jesus Christ live on earth?

A.

A life of suffering and poverty

PROVE IT !

Isaiah 53:3

Q.50 **What kind of death did Christ suffer?**

A. A painful and shameful death on the cross

PROVE IT !

Philippians 2:8

Q. 51

Does Christ Jesus still remain in his tomb?

A.

No, God raised him on the 3rd day.

PROVE IT !

1 Corinthians 15:4

Q. 52

Where is Jesus Christ today?

A.

In heaven seated in
the right hand of God
_____

PROVE IT !

Hebrews 1:3b

Q. 53

Will Christ Jesus return to earth?

A.

Yes, He will come to judge the world.

PROVE IT!

Revelation 22:12

Q. 54

How can I be redeemed?

A.

By the irresistible call of God

PROVE IT !

2 Timothy 1:9

Q. 55

What is the effective call?

A. God drawing sinners to Christ

_____

PROVE IT !

John 6:44

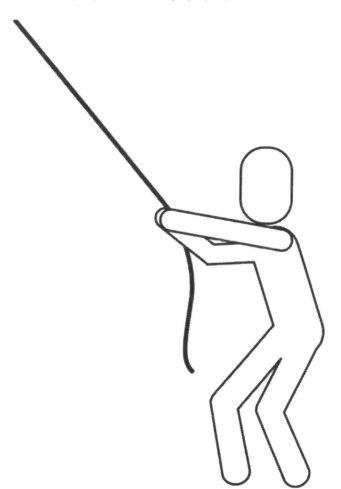

Q. 56 **How can sinners hear about Christ?**

A. In the gospel of Jesus Christ

PROVE IT !

John 3:16

Q. 57

What blessing do the called actually receive?

A.

Justification, adoption, and sanctification

PROVE IT !

1 Corinthians 1:30

Q. 58

What is justification?

A.

Declared righteous by
God

PROVE IT !
2 Corinthians 5:21

Q. 59

What is adoption?

A.

God welcomes sinners

into His family.

PROVE IT !

1 John 3:1a

Q. 60

What is sanctification?

A. Making sinners holy in heart and conduct.

PROVE IT !

1 Thessalonians 5:23

Q. 61

What happens to the justified when they die?

A.

Body returns to dust and spirit to the Lord

PROVE IT !

2 Corinthians 5:8

Q. 62

What happens to the unjust when they die?

A. Suffer punishment while waiting God's Judment.

PROVE IT !
Luke 16:22b-23a

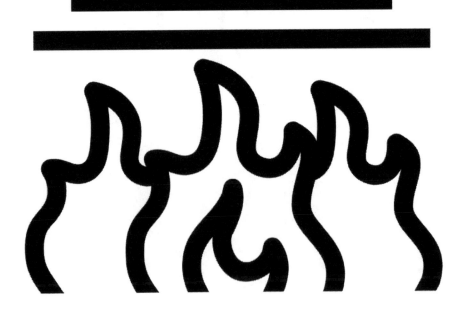

Q. 63

Will the dead rise?

A.

Yes, when

Jesus returns.

PROVE IT !

1 Thessalonians 4:16

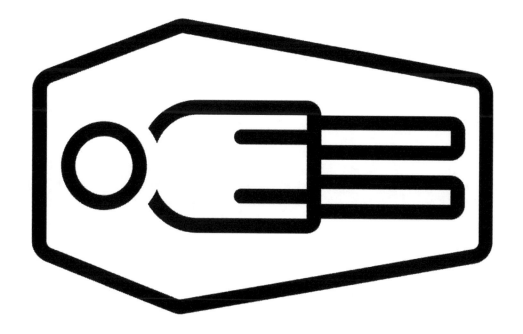

Q. 64

What will happen to the unjust on the day of judgment ?

A.

Be thrown into the lake of fire

PROVE IT !

Revelations 2015

Q. 65

What is the lake of fire?

A.
Place of eternal punishment.

PROVE IT !

Mark 9:48

Q. 66

What will happen to the righteous on the day of judgment ?

A. Will go to the new heaven and new earth.

PROVE IT !

Matthew 25:34

Q. 67   What is new heaven and new earth?

A. Where God and his people be will be forever.

PROVE IT !
Revelation 21:3

Q. 68
What does God require of man?

A. Obedience to His revealed will

PROVE IT !

Micah 6:8

Q. 69

What is the revealed will of God?

A.   In His holy Law.

PROVE IT !
Romans 7:12

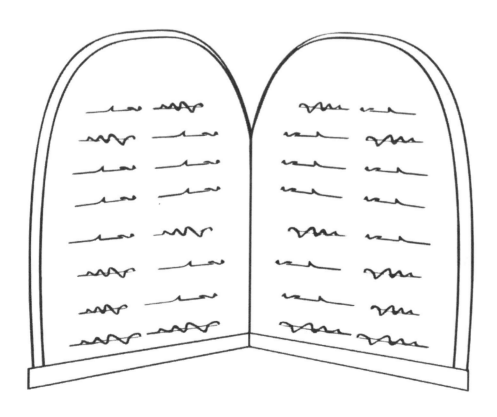

Q. 70

Where do we find God's law?

A.   In the 10 commandments

PROVE IT !

Deuteronomy 4:13

Q. 71

What is the summary of the 10 commandments ?

A.

Love the Lord and

your neighbor

PROVE IT !

Matthew 22 : 37-40

Q. 72

Who is your neighbor?

A.

Anyone around me.

PROVE IT !

Matthew 22:37-40

Q. 73

What is the first commandment?

A. You will have no other God.

PROVE IT !

Exodus 20:3

Q. 74

What does the first commandment teach us?

A.

Worship and serve only God

PROVE IT !

Matthew 4:10

Q. 75

What is the second commandment ?

A. "Have no idols in any way.

PROVE IT !

Exodus 20:4

Q. 76

What does the second commandment teach us?

A.

Worship only God and do not practice idolatry.

PROVE IT !

Deuteronomy 12:32

Q. 77

What is the third commandment ?

A.

Do not use God's

name in vain

PROVE IT !

Exodus 20:7

Q. 78 **What does the third commandment teach us?**

A. Have reverence for His name in words and deeds.

PROVE IT !

Revelation 15:3b-4a

Q. 79

What is the fourth commandment ?

A.   Remember the
Sabbath, keep it holy.

PROVE IT !
Exodus 20:8

Q. 80   **What does the fourth commandment teach us?**

A. Keeping the Lords day holy.

PROVE IT !

Exodus 20:8

Q. 81

What day of the week is the Christian sabbath?

A.

Sunday, the first day of the week called Lords day.

PROVE IT!

Acts 20:7

SUNDAY

Q. 82

Why do we call it the Lord's Day?

A. It is the day Jesus rose from the dead.

PROVE IT !

John 20:1

Q. 83
What do we do on the Lord's Day?

A.

Pray,worship, listen to Gods word.

PROVE IT !
Leviticus 23:3

Q. 84

What is the fifth commandment?

A.

Honor your father
and mother.

PROVE IT !
Exodus 20:12

Q. 85

What does the fifth commandment teach us?

A. To love, obey, and respect our

_____

parents.

PROVE IT!

Ephesians 6:1

Q. 86

What is the sixth commandment ?

A.

You shall not kill.

PROVE IT !

Exodus 2013

Q. 87

What does the sixth commandment teach us ?

A. To love with the heart, with words and conduct.

PROVE IT !
Psalm 82:3-4

Q. 88
What is the seventh commandment ?

A.   You shall not
commit adultery.

PROVE IT !
Exodus 20:14

Q. 89

What does the seventh commandment teach us?

A.

Be pure in heart,with words, and conduct

PROVE IT !

Ephesians 5:3-4b

Q. 90

What is the eight commandment ?

A.

You shall not steal.

PROVE IT !

Exodus 2015

Q. 91

What does the eighth commandment teach us?

A. Be honest and hardworking.

PROVE IT !

Ephesians 4:28

Q. 92

What is the ninth commandment ?

A.

You shall not lie.

PROVE IT !

Exodus 2016

Q. 93

What does the ninth commandment teach us?

A.

Tell the truth.

PROVE IT !

Proverbs 12:22

Q. 94

What's the tenth commandment ?

A.

You'll shall not covet.

PROVE IT !

Exodus 2017

Q. 95

What does the tenth commandment teach us?

A.

Be happy with what we do.

PROVE IT !

Hebrews 13:5

Q. 96   **Can any man fufill the 10 commandments perfectly?**

A. No man can or will since the fall of Adam.

PROVE IT !

Ecclesiastes 7:20

96

Q. 97   **What is the use of God's Commandments ?**

A. Teaches us our duty and need of Savior.

PROVE IT !

Romans 3:20

Q. 98

What does each sin deserve?

A.

God's wrath and curse.

PROVE IT !

Galatians 3:10

Q. 99

Who will escape the wrath of God?

A.

Only those who repent and believe in Jesus.

PROVE IT!
Joel 2:13

Q. 100   **What is repentance ?**

A.

Asking for forgiveness
and hating sin.

PROVE IT !

Joel 2

Q. 101 What is believing and
having faith in Christ?

A. Trust only in Christ
for salvation.

PROVE IT!
John 1:12

Q. 102

How many sacraments are there?

A. There are 2 Sacraments

PROVE IT!

Matthew 28: 18-19a

Q.103 What are the 2 sacraments

A. Baptism and the Lord's Supper

PROVE IT!

Matthew 28:18-19b

Q.104

Who ordained these sacraments?

A.   The Lord Jesus Christ.

PROVE IT!

Matthew 28:18-19b

Q. 105 Why did Christ ordain these sacraments?

A. To distinguish, encourage and strengthen His people.

PROVE IT!

1 Corinthians 11:23-26

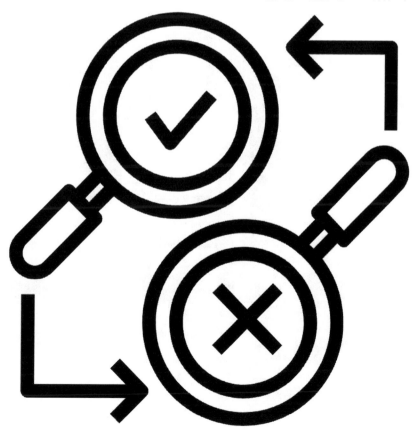

Q.106

How is the manner of Baptism?

A.   Submerged in water.

_____

PROVE IT!

John 3:23

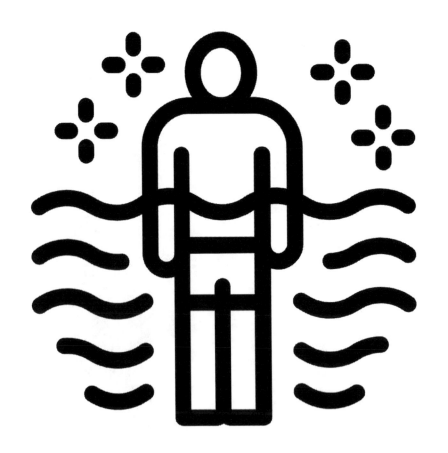

Q.107

What does baptism represent?

A.   Union with Jesus Christ.

PROVE IT!

Romans 6:3

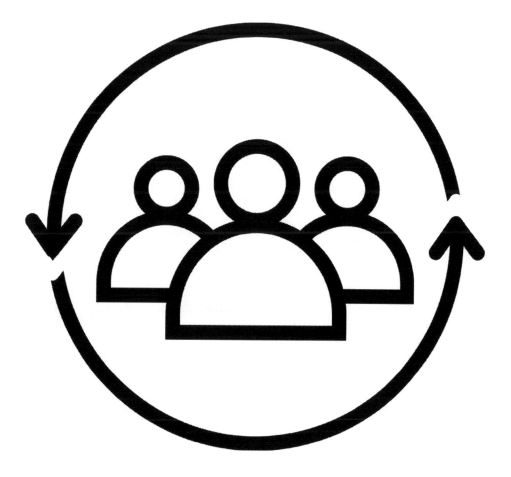

Q. 108

In whose name are we baptized?

A. In name of Father, Son, Holy Spirit.

PROVE IT!
Matthew 28:19

Q. 109 Who can be baptized?

A. Only believers.

PROVE IT!
Acts 2:41

Q. 110

To what does baptism bind you?

A.   To be a true
believer

PROVE IT!
Romans 6:4

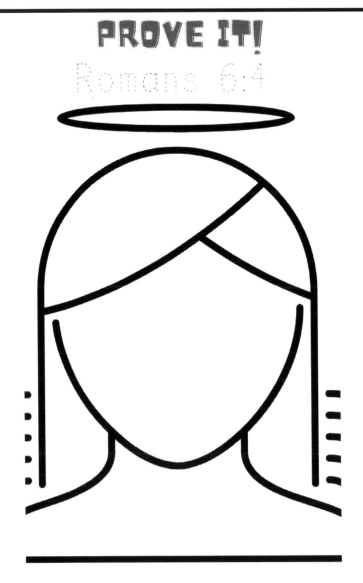

Q. III

What is the Lord's Supper?

A.

Eating bread and drinking
from cup in memory of
Christ death.

_____

PROVE IT!
Luke 22:19-20

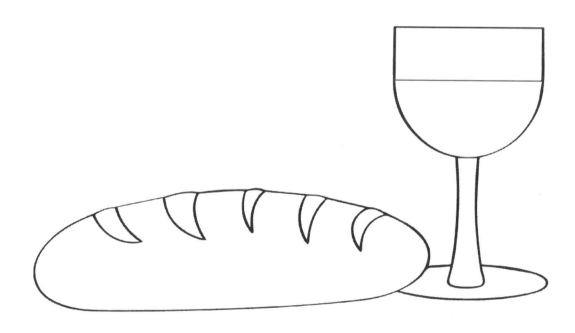

Q. 112

What does the cup represent?

A. The blood of Christ, shed for our sins

PROVE IT!
Luke 22:19-20

Q. 113

Who can take the Lord's table?

A. Only those who are believers

PROVE IT!

1 Corinthians 11:28-29

Q. 114

What is prayer?

A.　Asking God for things He has promised to give.

PROVE IT!

Ephesians 4:6

Q. 115

In whose name should we pray?

A.   Only in the name of Jesus Christ.

PROVE IT!

John 16: 23-24

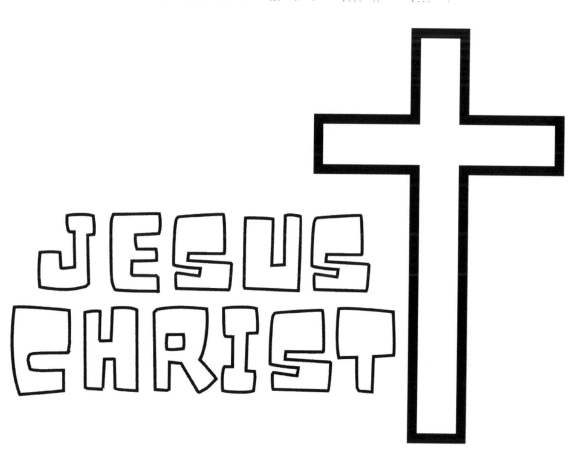

JESUS CHRIST

Q. 116

What has Christ given us to teach us how to pray?

A.

The Lord's Prayer.

PROVE IT!

Matthew 6: 9-13

Q. 117 Repeat the Lord's Prayer.

A.   Our Father in heaven, Holly be your name. Your kingdom come, your will be done on earth as it is in heaven. Give us today our daily bread and forgiven us our debts, as we have also forgiven our debtors. Do not let us fall into temptation, but keep us from evil. For yours is the kingdom and the power and the glory forever and ever. Amen.

PROVE IT!
Matthew 6:9-13

Q. 118

How many petitions are there in the Lord's Prayer?

A.

_____

PROVE IT!
Matthew 6:9-13

Q. 119

What is the first request?

A.

Holly be your name.

PROVE IT!

Matthew 6:9b

Q. 120

What do we pray in the first request?

A. God's name be honored by us and all men.

PROVE IT!
Psalm 67:3

Q. 121

What is the second request?

A.

Your kingdom come.

PROVE IT!

Matthew 6:10

Q. 122 What do we pray in the second request?

A. May the gospel be preached, believed and obeyed by us and all

PROVE IT!
2 Thessalonians 3:1

Q. 123

What is the third request?

A. Your will be done on earth as it is in heaven.

PROVE IT!

Matthew 6:10

Q. 124 What do we pray in the third request ?

A. That we serve God as the angels in heaven.

PROVE IT!

Psalm 103: 20-22

Q. 125

What is the fourth request?

A.   Give us today our daily bread.

PROVE IT!

Matthew 6:11

Q. 126

What do we pray in the fourth petition?

A. Give us the things we need for our body and souls.

PROVE IT!

Proverbs 30:8

Q. 127

What is the fifth petition?

A. Forgive our debts, as we forgive our debtors.

PROVE IT!

Matthew 6:12

127

Q. 128 What do we pray in the fifth petition?

A. God forgive our sins in Christ, and to help us to forgive.

PROVE IT!

1 John 1:9

Q. 129

What is the sixth petition ?

A. Do not let us fall into temptation.

PROVE IT!

Matthew 6:13

Q. 130

What do we pray in the sixth petition?

A.

That God save us from

sin.

PROVE IT!

Psalm 19:13

☐Published by Editorial Credo, Oklahoma, City OK |

Shorter Baptist Catechism Work Book (Tracing and coloring) Copyright ©2021 by Karen Vazquez- Salas.

Cover illustration by Karen Vazquez-Salas Cover design by Karen Vazquez- Salas. Interior layout by Juan Salas.

Printed in the United States of America.

Karen Vázquez-Salas. Shorter Baptist Catechism, Editorial Credo, OKLAHOMA CITY OK.

☐

Shorter Baptist Catechism Work Book (Tracing and coloring) Copyright ©2021 by Karen Vazquez- Salas.

Made in the USA
Middletown, DE
31 October 2023

41713995R00075